A CHILD'S GUIDE TO
WISDOM

EVERTON ROBINSON

Third Edition

This book is a work of fiction. Places, events, and situations in this story are purely fictional. Any resemblance to actual persons, living or dead is coincidental.

CPSIA information can be obtained
at www.ICGTesting.com
FSOW03n0359060116
15370FS

Luaurcan Publishing, LLC
5491 Fox Hills Avenue
Buena Park, CA 90621

Telephone: 1(714) 461-2383
Fax: 1(714) 441-8789

Ordering Information:
Quantity sales. Special discounts are available on quantity purchases by corporations, associations, and others. For details, contact the publisher at the address above.

Printed in the United States of America.

ISBN-13: 978-1-09831-214-5

ACKNOWLEDGEMENTS

I would like to acknowledge a few persons who have been instrumental in the publishing of this book:

- First and foremost, I want to give thanks to Almighty God, who is the source of all wisdom and the Lord of my life.

- My wife, Judith Jones-Robinson, my pillar of strength and support, who suggested that I write the book; as she observed me constantly instructing, repeating and drilling our twin daughters on the principles in this book. Judith also reviewed and corrected the manuscript and forced me to strive for excellence in the formatting and appearance of the book.

- My twin daughters, Candace and Lauren, who were my test cases in determining the effectiveness of the concept of this book. From the time they could speak, I began to teach them the principles of wisdom by effective repetition. As they grew, they could recite the principles from memory, although initially, they did not always understand the meaning. However over time, as the girls matured, the meaning became clearer and clearer. It is through this process that Candace and Lauren have embraced wisdom as a philosophy and way of life; and as a result, have become two of the finest and wisest young ladies you would ever want to meet.

INTRODUCTION

Dear Parent or Guardian,

If as a child you had the wisdom you now possess as an adult, do you believe that your life would be different? Do you believe you would be much more successful than you are right now? I think I speak for all of us when I respond to these questions with an overwhelming **YES!**

We cannot go back and relive the past, but we can certainly impart the wisdom we have gained to our children and grandchildren, in hopes that they may enjoy its tremendous benefits. That is why this book was written. In addition, I know that this system works, because I used it to rear my twin daughters; and they have become two of the wisest young ladies you would ever want to meet.

One more question to consider: If you had to choose between having an educated child or a wise child, which would you choose? If you really think about it, you would want your child to be wise. Why? Because based on the definition of wisdom, a wise child would choose to be educated. However, an educated child may or may not choose to be wise. This is evidenced in the thousands of young people who leave colleges and universities with an education, only to ruin their lives because of the unwise choices they make. My conclusion is that there are all kinds of educational institutions, but I have yet to find one specifically designed to teach the principles of wisdom.

The purpose of this book is as follows:

1. To pass on words of wisdom to your children;
2. To provide adults with a tool to teach wisdom to children;
3. To teach children the value of earning money by putting forth effort to learn wisdom;

4. To provide an alternative for giving allowance to children;
5. To teach children that wisdom pays big dividends;
6. To help children to become better citizens of the world.

Research has shown that it takes 21 repetitions of a thought or action to form a habit. This research forms the basis of the compensation system I have developed, which is geared to motivate the child to quote the principle from memory a minimum of 21 times. Each time the child quotes the principle from memory, you should initial the chart and pay him/her the amount of compensation you have agreed to pay for each quotation mastered. I have also included a perseverance bonus to motivate the child to complete the memorization process, and I have left the amount of the bonus to be earned up to you. I have also included a certification section so that upon completion, you may sign it, remove the page, frame it, and place it on the wall in the child's room as sign of accomplishment.

Two other very important matters I must emphasize. It is not enough just to hand this book to your child. In order to achieve the maximum results, the parent or guardian must be actively involved in the teaching/learning process. Furthermore, I want to point out that repetition alone is not enough. You must instill in the child the importance of practicing the principles of wisdom. During the time when my children were growing up, my wife and I would constantly point-out everyday instances and examples of the use of or absence of a certain wisdom principle. "What would wisdom dictate?" would be our resounding question. Or we would ask, "What wisdom principle is present (or missing)?" in a particular everyday circumstance.

It is my earnest belief that if you take the time to teach these principles to the children around you, you will be making a significant contribution toward making the world a better place, by developing future men and women of good character, strong integrity, and wisdom.

From the time of birth until the child is about five years old, you as a parent or guardian have a very narrow window of sole influence to impact the child's thinking and perspective. It is up to you to take full advantage of this opportunity to shape their minds by planting the seeds of wisdom through these principles.

The explanations of the principles presented in this book are not comprehensive. Rather, they are intended to give the child a working definition that he or she can relate to and memorize.

HOW TO USE THIS BOOK

The following recommendations are hereby offered for optimal use of the book:

For The Family

1. Husband and wife or Guardian should make a decision to embrace wisdom as a way of life.

2. Select a principle for each week.

3. Do the following around the dinner table daily:

    Repeat the following affirmation:

    a. "We the _____ Family hereby affirm that we embrace Wisdom as our way of life. We will walk in Wisdom, talk with Wisdom, and do all we do with Wisdom as our guide."

    b. In a 'call and repeat' manner, quote the principle of the day three times. Dad should lead on the first day, Mom the second day and the children in turn on the remaining days if they can. The rotation should continue throughout the week. That means that the whole family will hear the principle 42 times in a week. By the end of the week, everyone will know the principle from memory.

    c.   Parents can clarify the principles with examples.

    d.   Ask children which principles they applied during the day.

For the Parent or Guardian

1. During story time, repeat the principle of the week three more times through the 'call and repeat' method.   his means the children will have heard the principle 42 times in addition to the dinner time repetitions.

2. As you watch television together, point out principles at work, and quiz your children about principles at work or principles violated in the television shows.

3. As you drive the children around in your car, ask them to define the current as well as previous principles.

4. As you see the principles at work or violated in life, point them out.

5. As the children quote the principles from memory, initial each number in the 1 to 21 sequence on the page of the principle in the book. You may set in place a reward system by agreeing to compensate the child in an agreed upon amount (a nickel, a dime, etc.), and have them put the payment in a "Wisdom Piggy Bank".

6. Use money from the "Wisdom Piggy Bank" from time-to-time to buy the child goodies. In this way, the child can see the correlation between wisdom, money, and goodies.

7. When the child has quoted the principle 21 times from memory, download the certificate for the principle from www.achildsguide-towisdom.net onto certificate stationery, and place it in a separate binder, or on a designated "Wall of Wisdom" in your home. Also, sign the certification at the bottom of the page and give the child a bonus, if appropriate.

8. In lieu of allowance, or when the child asks for money, have the child quote principles in order to **earn** the money they are requesting.

This works for teenagers as well.

For Grandparents

This is the least expensive way to leave a lasting legacy for future generations. Leave them the Gift of Wisdom. Since it is the prerogative of grandparents to spoil their grandchildren, I recommend that you make wisdom a basis for spoiling them.

1. If the parents of the children are implementing the program, the grandparents may re-enforce the teachings by compensating the grandchildren based on the child's scores given by the parents. For example, if the parent gives the child a dime for each principle quoted from memory, the grandparents can give them the same amount, or a different amount based on the number of times the child has quoted the principles to their parents.

2. Before you spoil them with any material or monetary gifts, have them quote principles to you. (Since you are going to give them the money anyway, why not use it to motivate them to learn wisdom!)

3. Give them a bonus whenever their parents give them a bonus for quoting the principle 21 times.

4. If the parents are not involved, get a book for each child and follow the directions in the "For the Parent or Guardian" section of these instructions.

For The School or Classroom

A Child's Guide to Wisdom can be used as a character-building tool in any school or classroom, and will serve as a value-added element for daily instruction. Embracing wisdom as a way of life in the school can result in well-rounded students, thus elevating the standards of the school, and commanding higher tuition. Here are some suggestions:

1. Include the following affirmation in the school's or classroom's daily ritual:

2. "We, the students of _____ School, hereby affirm that we embrace Wisdom as our way of life. We will walk in Wisdom, talk with Wisdom, and do all we do with Wisdom as our guide."

3. Have the parents purchase a book for each child, so that they can monitor the child's progress and compensate them. For this, follow the steps in the "For the Parent or Guardian" section of these instructions.

4. Select a principle of the week.

5. Select a time of the day when the principle will be taught.

6. During the specific time, repeat the principle 5 times through call and repeat. (This means the students will hear the principle 10 times a day, 5 days a week. By the end of the week, they will know the principle from memory.)

7. Have discussion and instruction on the principle of the week.

8. Quiz the students for prior weeks' principles, and give "On The Spot" awards.

9. Have contests using the principles.

10. Designate a wall in the school or classroom as the "Wall of Wisdom"

11. Issue certificates when the student masters the principles; and display the certificates on the "Wall of Wisdom".

The point of the whole process is to plant and water the seeds of wisdom in the mind of the child, and allow the child to grow into the knowledge and awareness of wisdom as he or she matures. The wisest man in the world--King Solomon--said this about Wisdom:

CHERISH HER [WISDOM], AND SHE WILL EXALT YOU;
EMBRACE HER, AND SHE WILL HONOR YOU.
SHE WILL GIVE YOU A GARLAND TO GRACE YOUR HEAD
AND PRESENT YOU WITH A GLORIOUS CROWN."

—PROVERBS 4:8-9 (NIV)

TABLE OF CONTENTS

"THE FEAR OF THE LORD IS THE BEGINNING OF KNOWLEDGE, BUT FOOLS DESPISE WISDOM AND DISCIPLINE."

PROVERBS 1:7 (NIV)

ACCOUNTABILITY

Is

Being good

For your word.

Wisdom Payment Chart

Every time you quote this principle from memory, you will earn_____.

(5c, 10c, 25c, etc.)

1 2 3 4 5 6 7 8 9 10 11 12 13 14 15 16 17 18 19 20 21
(Adult to initial number representing the number of times quoted.)

Certification

I_____hereby certify that_____has quoted this principle from memory 21 times, and is therefore entitled to the perseverance bonus of $_____.

_____
Signature

ACTION

Is

Doing something

Even if you are not completely sure.

<u>Wisdom Payment Chart</u>

Every time you quote this principle from memory, you will earn_____.

(5c, 10c, 25c, etc.)

1 2 3 4 5 6 7 8 9 10 11 12 13 14 15 16 17 18 19 20 21
(Adult to initial number representing the number of times quoted.)

Certification

I_____hereby certify that_____has quoted this principle from memory, 21 times, and is therefore entitled to the <u>perseverance bonus</u> of $_____.

_____
Signature

AWARENESS

Is

Being tuned into

The world about you.

<u>Wisdom Payment Chart</u>

Every time you quote this principle from memory, you will earn_____.

(5c, 10c, 25c, etc.)

1 2 3 4 5 6 7 8 9 10 11 12 13 14 15 16 17 18 19 20 21

(Adult to initial number representing the number of times quoted.)

Certification

I_____hereby certify that_____has quoted this principle from memory 21 times, and is therefore entitled to the <u>perseverance bonus</u> of $_____.

_____

Signature

CHARACTER

Is

Doing the right things

The right way.

Wisdom Payment Chart

Every time you quote this principle from memory, you will earn_____.

(5c, 10c, 25c, etc.)

1 2 3 4 5 6 7 8 9 10 11 12 13 14 15 16 17 18 19 20 21

(Adult to initial number representing the number of times quoted.)

Certification

I_____hereby certify that_____has quoted
this principle from memory 21 times, and is therefore entitled to the
perseverance bonus of $_____.

_____
      Signature

CONSISTENCY

Is

Doing the same things

the same way.

Wisdom Payment Chart

Every time you quote this principle from memory, you will earn_____.

(5c, 10c, 25c, etc.)

1 2 3 4 5 6 7 8 9 10 11 12 13 14 15 16 17 18 19 20 21
(Adult to initial number representing the number of times quoted.)

Certification

I_____hereby certify that_____has quoted this principle from memory 21 times, and is therefore entitled to the perseverance bonus of $_____.

_____
     Signature

COURAGE

Is

Doing what you are supposed to do

Even

When you are afraid to do it.

Wisdom Payment Chart

Every time you quote this principle from memory, you will earn_____.

(5c, 10c, 25c, etc.)

1 2 3 4 5 6 7 8 9 10 11 12 13 14 15 16 17 18 19 20 21
(Adult to initial number representing the number of times quoted.)

Certification

I_____hereby certify that_____has quoted this principle from memory 21 times, and is therefore entitled to the perseverance bonus of $_____.

_____
Signature

COURTESY

Is

Treating others

In a respectful manner.

<u>Wisdom Payment Chart</u>

Every time you quote this principle from memory, you will earn_____.

(5c, 10c, 25c, etc.)

1 2 3 4 5 6 7 8 9 10 11 12 13 14 15 16 17 18 19 20 21
(Adult to initial number representing the number of times quoted.)

<u>Certification</u>

I_____hereby certify that_____has quoted this principle from memory 21 times, and is therefore entitled to the <u>perseverance bonus</u> of $_____.

_____
Signature

CREATIVITY

Is

Finding new ways

To get things done.

Wisdom Payment Chart

Every time you quote this principle from memory, you will earn_____.

(5c, 10c, 25c, etc.)

1 2 3 4 5 6 7 8 9 10 11 12 13 14 15 16 17 18 19 20 21
(Adult to initial number representing the number of times quoted.)

Certification

I_____hereby certify that_____has quoted this principle from memory 21 times, and is therefore entitled to the perseverance bonus of $_____.

_____
Signature

DISCIPLINE

Is

Doing what you are supposed to do

Even

When you don't feel like doing it.

<u>Wisdom Payment Chart</u>

Every time you quote this principle from memory, you will earn_____.

(5c, 10c, 25c, etc.)

1 2 3 4 5 6 7 8 9 10 11 12 13 14 15 16 17 18 19 20 21
(Adult to initial number representing the number of times quoted.)

Certification

I_____hereby certify that_____has quoted this principle from memory 21 times, and is therefore entitled to the <u>perseverance bonus</u> of $_____.

_____
Signature

EDIFICATION

Is

Building

Another person up.

Wisdom Payment Chart

Every time you quote this principle from memory, you will earn_____.

(5c, 10c, 25c, etc.)

1 2 3 4 5 6 7 8 9 10 11 12 13 14 15 16 17 18 19 20 21
(Adult to initial number representing the number of times quoted.)

Certification

I_____hereby certify that_____has quoted this principle from memory 21 times, and is therefore entitled to the perseverance bonus of $_____.

_____
Signature

ENTHUSIASM

Is

The positive energy

That comes from

God within.

<u>Wisdom Payment Chart</u>

Every time you quote this principle from memory, you will earn_____.

(5c, 10c, 25c, etc.)

1 2 3 4 5 6 7 8 9 10 11 12 13 14 15 16 17 18 19 20 21
(Adult to initial number representing the number of times quoted.)

Certification

I_____hereby certify that_____has quoted this principle from memory 21 times, and is therefore entitled to the <u>perseverance bonus</u> of $_____.

_____
Signature

EXCELLENCE

Is

Doing things in an

Outstandingly good way.

<u>Wisdom Payment Chart</u>

Every time you quote this principle from memory, you will earn_____.

(5c, 10c, 25c, etc.)

1 2 3 4 5 6 7 8 9 10 11 12 13 14 15 16 17 18 19 20 21
(Adult to initial number representing the number of times quoted.)

<u>Certification</u>

I_____hereby certify that_____has quoted
this principle from memory 21 times, and is therefore entitled to the
<u>perseverance bonus</u> of $_____.

_____
        Signature

FAIRNESS

Is

Giving to each person
What they have earned.

Wisdom Payment Chart

Every time you quote this principle from memory, you will earn_____.

(5c, 10c, 25c, etc.)

1 2 3 4 5 6 7 8 9 10 11 12 13 14 15 16 17 18 19 20 21
(Adult to initial number representing the number of times quoted.)

Certification

I_____hereby certify that_____has quoted this principle from memory 21 times, and is therefore entitled to the perseverance bonus of $_____.

_____
Signature

FAITH

Is

Knowing that you will

Have what you want,

Even if you don't yet see it.

Wisdom Payment Chart

Every time you quote this principle from memory, you will earn_____.

(5c, 10c, 25c, etc.)

1 2 3 4 5 6 7 8 9 10 11 12 13 14 15 16 17 18 19 20 21
(Adult to initial number representing the number of times quoted.)

Certification

I_____hereby certify that_____has quoted
this principle from memory 21 times, and is therefore entitled to the
perseverance bonus of $_____.

_____
    Signature

FORGIVENESS

Is

Not holding other people's

Bad behavior

Against them.

Wisdom Payment Chart

Every time you quote this principle from memory, you will earn_____.

(5c, 10c, 25c, etc.)

1 2 3 4 5 6 7 8 9 10 11 12 13 14 15 16 17 18 19 20 21
(Adult to initial number representing the number of times quoted.)

Certification

I_____hereby certify that_____has quoted this principle from memory 21 times, and is therefore entitled to the perseverance bonus of $_____.

_____
      Signature

GIVING

Is

Willingly

Letting another person

Have what belongs to you.

Wisdom Payment Chart

Every time you quote this principle from memory, you will earn_____.

(5c, 10c, 25c, etc.)

1 2 3 4 5 6 7 8 9 10 11 12 13 14 15 16 17 18 19 20 21

(Adult to initial number representing the number of times quoted.)

Certification

I_____hereby certify that_____has quoted this principle from memory 21 times, and is therefore entitled to the perseverance bonus of $_____.

_____
Signature

HONESTY

Is

Being truthful

In

Thought, word, and deed.

Wisdom Payment Chart

Every time you quote this principle from memory, you will earn_____.

(5c, 10c, 25c, etc.)

1 2 3 4 5 6 7 8 9 10 11 12 13 14 15 16 17 18 19 20 21
(Adult to initial number representing the number of times quoted.)

Certification

I_____hereby certify that_____has quoted this principle from memory 21 times, and is therefore entitled to the <u>perseverance bonus</u> of $_____.

_____
Signature

HUMILITY

Is

Not making

A big deal

Of yourself

Wisdom Payment Chart

Every time you quote this principle from memory, you will earn_____.

(5c, 10c, 25c, etc.)

1 2 3 4 5 6 7 8 9 10 11 12 13 14 15 16 17 18 19 20 21
(Adult to initial number representing the number of times quoted.)

Certification

I_____hereby certify that_____has quoted
this principle from memory 21 times, and is therefore entitled to the
perseverance bonus of $_____.

_____
Signature

INNER STRENGTH

Is

Knowing

That you have what it takes,

And acting on it.

<u>Wisdom Payment Chart</u>

Every time you quote this principle from memory, you will earn_____.

(5c, 10c, 25c, etc.)

1 2 3 4 5 6 7 8 9 10 11 12 13 14 15 16 17 18 19 20 21

(Adult to initial number representing the number of times quoted.)

<u>Certification</u>

I_____hereby certify that_____has quoted this principle from memory 21 times, and is therefore entitled to the <u>perseverance bonus</u> of $_____.

_____

Signature

INTEGRITY

Is

Doing the right thing

Even

If it costs you.

Wisdom Payment Chart

Every time you quote this principle from memory, you will earn_____.
(5c, 10c, 25c, etc.)

1 2 3 4 5 6 7 8 9 10 11 12 13 14 15 16 17 18 19 20 21
(Adult to initial number representing the number of times quoted.)

Certification

I_____hereby certify that_____has quoted this principle from memory 21 times, and is therefore entitled to the perseverance bonus of $_____.

_____
Signature

JUSTICE

Is

Giving to others

What they deserve.

Wisdom Payment Chart

Every time you quote this principle from memory, you will earn_____.

(5c, 10c, 25c, etc.)

1 2 3 4 5 6 7 8 9 10 11 12 13 14 15 16 17 18 19 20 21
(Adult to initial number representing the number of times quoted.)

Certification

I_____hereby certify that_____has quoted this principle from memory 21 times, and is therefore entitled to the perseverance bonus of $_____.

_____
Signature

KNOWLEDGE

Is

Having the information you need

To do

What you are supposed to do.

<u>Wisdom Payment Chart</u>

Every time you quote this principle from memory, you will earn_____.

(5c, 10c, 25c, etc.)

1 2 3 4 5 6 7 8 9 10 11 12 13 14 15 16 17 18 19 20 21
(Adult to initial number representing the number of times quoted.)

<u>Certification</u>

I_____hereby certify that_____has quoted
this principle from memory 21 times, and is therefore entitled to the
<u>perseverance bonus</u> of $_____.

_____
Signature

LAUGHTER

Is

The sound that comes from

Making someone happy.

Wisdom Payment Chart

Every time you quote this principle from memory, you will earn_____.

(5c, 10c, 25c, etc.)

1 2 3 4 5 6 7 8 9 10 11 12 13 14 15 16 17 18 19 20 21
(Adult to initial number representing the number of times quoted.)

Certification

I_____hereby certify that_____has quoted this principle from memory 21 times, and is therefore entitled to the perseverance bonus of $_____.

_____
Signature

LOVE

Is

Giving

Of

Yourself.

Wisdom Payment Chart

Every time you quote this principle from memory, you will earn_____.

(5c, 10c, 25c, etc.)

1 2 3 4 5 6 7 8 9 10 11 12 13 14 15 16 17 18 19 20 21

(Adult to initial number representing the number of times quoted.)

Certification

I_____hereby certify that_____has quoted this principle from memory 21 times, and is therefore entitled to the perseverance bonus of $_____.

_____

     Signature

MENTORSHIP

Is

Learning from

Another person's experience.

Wisdom Payment Chart

Every time you quote this principle from memory, you will earn_____.

(5c, 10c, 25c, etc.)

1 2 3 4 5 6 7 8 9 10 11 12 13 14 15 16 17 18 19 20 21
(Adult to initial number representing the number of times quoted.)

Certification

I_____hereby certify that_____has quoted
this principle from memory 21 times, and is therefore entitled to the
perseverance bonus of $_____.

_____
Signature

MERCY

Is

Not giving others

The punishment they deserve.

Wisdom Payment Chart

Every time you quote this principle from memory, you will earn_____.

(5c, 10c, 25c, etc.)

1 2 3 4 5 6 7 8 9 10 11 12 13 14 15 16 17 18 19 20 21
(Adult to initial number representing the number of times quoted.)

Certification

I_____hereby certify that_____has quoted this principle from memory 21 times, and is therefore entitled to the perseverance bonus of $_____.

_____
Signature

MODESTY

Is

Not making a big deal

Of your success.

Wisdom Payment Chart

Every time you quote this principle from memory, you will earn_____.

(5c, 10c, 25c, etc.)

1 2 3 4 5 6 7 8 9 10 11 12 13 14 15 16 17 18 19 20 21
(Adult to initial number representing the number of times quoted.)

Certification

I_____hereby certify that_____has quoted this principle from memory 21 times, and is therefore entitled to the perseverance bonus of $_____.

_____
Signature

OBEDIENCE

Is

Doing what you are told,

When you are told,

The first time you're told.

<u>Wisdom Payment Chart</u>

Every time you quote this principle from memory, you will earn_____.

(5c, 10c, 25c, etc.)

1 2 3 4 5 6 7 8 9 10 11 12 13 14 15 16 17 18 19 20 21
(Adult to initial number representing the number of times quoted.)

<u>Certification</u>

I_____hereby certify that_____has quoted this principle from memory 21 times, and is therefore entitled to the <u>perseverance bonus</u> of $_____.

_____
Signature

OPTIMISM

Is

Believing in a

Positive outcome.

<u>Wisdom Payment Chart</u>

Every time you quote this principle from memory, you will earn_____.

(5c, 10c, 25c, etc.)

1 2 3 4 5 6 7 8 9 10 11 12 13 14 15 16 17 18 19 20 21
(Adult to initial number representing the number of times quoted.)

<u>Certification</u>

I_____hereby certify that_____has quoted
this principle from memory 21 times, and is therefore entitled to the
<u>perseverance bonus</u> of $_____.

_____
     Signature

PASSION

Is

Doing what you do

With all your heart.

Wisdom Payment Chart

Every time you quote this principle from memory, you will earn_____.

(5c, 10c, 25c, etc.)

1 2 3 4 5 6 7 8 9 10 11 12 13 14 15 16 17 18 19 20 21
(Adult to initial number representing the number of times quoted.)

Certification

I_____hereby certify that_____has quoted
this principle from memory 21 times, and is therefore entitled to the
perseverance bonus of $_____.

_____
      Signature

PATIENCE

Is

Waiting for what you want,

Knowing that you will get it.

Wisdom Payment Chart

Every time you quote this principle from memory, you will earn_____.

(5c, 10c, 25c, etc.)

1 2 3 4 5 6 7 8 9 10 11 12 13 14 15 16 17 18 19 20 21
(Adult to initial number representing the number of times quoted.)

Certification

I_____hereby certify that_____has quoted this principle from memory 21 times, and is therefore entitled to the perseverance bonus of $_____.

_____
      Signature

PERSEVERANCE

Is

Persistence under

The most severe

Conditions.

Wisdom Payment Chart

Every time you quote this principle from memory, you will earn_____.

(5c, 10c, 25c, etc.)

1 2 3 4 5 6 7 8 9 10 11 12 13 14 15 16 17 18 19 20 21
(Adult to initial number representing the number of times quoted.)

Certification

I_____hereby certify that_____has quoted this principle from memory 21 times, and is therefore entitled to the perseverance bonus of $_____.

_____
Signature

PERSISTENCE

Is

Trying one more time

Than you fail.

Wisdom Payment Chart

Every time you quote this principle from memory, you will earn_____.

(5c, 10c, 25c, etc.)

1 2 3 4 5 6 7 8 9 10 11 12 13 14 15 16 17 18 19 20 21

(Adult to initial number representing the number of times quoted.)

Certification

I_____hereby certify that_____has quoted this principle from memory 21 times, and is therefore entitled to the perseverance bonus of $_____.

_____

Signature

POLITENESS

Is

Doing and saying things

In a kind way.

Wisdom Payment Chart

Every time you quote this principle from memory, you will earn_____.

(5c, 10c, 25c, etc.)

1 2 3 4 5 6 7 8 9 10 11 12 13 14 15 16 17 18 19 20 21

(Adult to initial number representing the number of times quoted.)

Certification

I_____hereby certify that_____has quoted this principle from memory 21 times, and is therefore entitled to the perseverance bonus of $_____.

_____

Signature

POSITIVE MENTAL ATTITUDE

Is

Knowing that everything

Is going to be all right.

Wisdom Payment Chart

Every time you quote this principle from memory, you will earn_____.

(5c, 10c, 25c, etc.)

1 2 3 4 5 6 7 8 9 10 11 12 13 14 15 16 17 18 19 20 21
(Adult to initial number representing the number of times quoted.)

Certification

I_____hereby certify that_____has quoted this principle from memory 21 times, and is therefore entitled to the perseverance bonus of $_____.

_____
       Signature

PRUDENCE

Is

Using

Good

Judgement.

Wisdom Payment Chart

Every time you quote this principle from memory, you will earn_____.

(5c, 10c, 25c, etc.)

1 2 3 4 5 6 7 8 9 10 11 12 13 14 15 16 17 18 19 20 21
(Adult to initial number representing the number of times quoted.)

Certification

I_____hereby certify that_____has quoted this principle from memory 21 times, and is therefore entitled to the perseverance bonus of $_____.

_____
Signature

PUNCTUALITY

Is

Being where you need to be

On time.

<u>Wisdom Payment Chart</u>

Every time you quote this principle from memory, you will earn_____.

(5c, 10c, 25c, etc.)

1 2 3 4 5 6 7 8 9 10 11 12 13 14 15 16 17 18 19 20 21
(Adult to initial number representing the number of times quoted.)

<u>Certification</u>

I_____hereby certify that_____has quoted this principle from memory 21 times, and is therefore entitled to the <u>perseverance bonus</u> of $_____.

_____

Signature

RESPECT

Is

Recognizing the greatness

In yourself

And others.

<u>Wisdom Payment Chart</u>

Every time you quote this principle from memory, you will earn_____.

(5c, 10c, 25c, etc.)

1 2 3 4 5 6 7 8 9 10 11 12 13 14 15 16 17 18 19 20 21
(Adult to initial number representing the number of times quoted.)

Certification

I_____hereby certify that_____has quoted this principle from memory 21 times, and is therefore entitled to the <u>perseverance bonus</u> of $_____.

_____
Signature

RESPONSIBILITY

Is

Looking to yourself

To get something done.

Wisdom Payment Chart

Every time you quote this principle from memory, you will earn_____.

(5c, 10c, 25c, etc.)

1 2 3 4 5 6 7 8 9 10 11 12 13 14 15 16 17 18 19 20 21
(Adult to initial number representing the number of times quoted.)

Certification

I_____hereby certify that_____has quoted
this principle from memory **21 times**, and is therefore entitled to the
perseverance bonus of $_____.

_____
Signature

SACRIFICE

Is

Giving up something

That is important to you

For something better.

Wisdom Payment Chart

Every time you quote this principle from memory, you will earn_____.

(5c, 10c, 25c, etc.)

1 2 3 4 5 6 7 8 9 10 11 12 13 14 15 16 17 18 19 20 21

(Adult to initial number representing the number of times quoted.)

Certification

I_____hereby certify that_____has quoted this principle from memory 21 times, and is therefore entitled to the perseverance bonus of $_____.

_____

Signature

SELF ESTEEM

Is

Seeing yourself

The way God sees you.

<u>Wisdom Payment Chart</u>

Every time you quote this principle from memory, you will earn_____.

(5c, 10c, 25c, etc.)

1 2 3 4 5 6 7 8 9 10 11 12 13 14 15 16 17 18 19 20 21
(Adult to initial number representing the number of times quoted.)

<u>Certification</u>

I_____hereby certify that_____has quoted
this principle from memory 21 times, and is therefore entitled to the
<u>perseverance bonus</u> of $_____.

_____
    Signature

SERENDIPITY

Is

The unexpected blessing

God gives you

For trying.

<u>Wisdom Payment Chart</u>

Every time you quote this principle from memory, you will earn_____.

(5c, 10c, 25c, etc.)

1 2 3 4 5 6 7 8 9 10 11 12 13 14 15 16 17 18 19 20 21

(Adult to initial number representing the number of times quoted.)

<u>Certification</u>

I_____hereby certify that_____has quoted this principle from memory 21 times, and is therefore entitled to the <u>perseverance bonus</u> of $_____.

_____

Signature

SERVICE

Is

Doing something

To help others.

<u>Wisdom Payment Chart</u>

Every time you quote this principle from memory, you will earn_____.

(5c, 10c, 25c, etc.)

1 2 3 4 5 6 7 8 9 10 11 12 13 14 15 16 17 18 19 20 21
(Adult to initial number representing the number of times quoted.)

<u>Certification</u>

I_____hereby certify that_____has quoted this principle from memory 21 times, and is therefore entitled to the <u>perseverance bonus</u> of $_____.

_____
Signature

SUBMISSION

Is

Allowing another person

To lead you.

Wisdom Payment Chart

Every time you quote this principle from memory, you will earn_____.

(5c, 10c, 25c, etc.)

1 2 3 4 5 6 7 8 9 10 11 12 13 14 15 16 17 18 19 20 21

(Adult to initial number representing the number of times quoted.)

Certification

I_____hereby certify that_____has quoted this principle from memory 21 times, and is therefore entitled to the perseverance bonus of $_____.

_____
Signature

SUCCESS

Is

Dreaming and

Making your dreams

Come true.

<u>Wisdom Payment Chart</u>

Every time you quote this principle from memory, you will earn_____.

(5c, 10c, 25c, etc.)

1 2 3 4 5 6 7 8 9 10 11 12 13 14 15 16 17 18 19 20 21
(Adult to initial number representing the number of times quoted.)

Certification

I_____hereby certify that_____has quoted this principle from memory **21 times**, and is therefore entitled to the <u>perseverance bonus</u> of $_____.

_____
Signature

TRANSPARENCY

Is

Being the same person

In public

That you are

In private.

Wisdom Payment Chart

Every time you quote this principle from memory, you will earn_____.

(5c, 10c, 25c, etc.)

1 2 3 4 5 6 7 8 9 10 11 12 13 14 15 16 17 18 19 20 21

(Adult to initial number representing the number of times quoted.)

Certification

I_____hereby certify that_____has quoted this principle from memory 21 times, and is therefore entitled to the perseverance bonus of $_____.

_____

Signature

UNDERSTANDING

Is

Making sense

Out of knowledge.

Wisdom Payment Chart

Every time you quote this principle from memory, you will earn_____.

(5c, 10c, 25c, etc.)

1 2 3 4 5 6 7 8 9 10 11 12 13 14 15 16 17 18 19 20 21
(Adult to initial number representing the number of times quoted.)

Certification

I_____hereby certify that_____has quoted this principle from memory **21 times**, and is therefore entitled to the perseverance bonus of $_____.

_____

Signature

VISION

Is

Seeing things that don't exist now,

But will exist in the future

As a result of your hard work

And God's help.

Wisdom Payment Chart

Every time you quote this principle from memory, you will earn_____.

(5c, 10c, 25c, etc.)

1 2 3 4 5 6 7 8 9 10 11 12 13 14 15 16 17 18 19 20 21
(Adult to initial number representing the number of times quoted.)

Certification

I_____hereby certify that_____has quoted
this principle from memory 21 times, and is therefore entitled to the
<u>perseverance bonus</u> of $_____.

_____
Signature

WISDOM

Is

Knowing what to do and

Doing it when you are supposed to do it,

And knowing what not to do

And not doing it.

<u>Wisdom Payment Chart</u>

Every time you quote this principle from memory, you will earn_____.

(5c, 10c, 25c, etc.)

1 2 3 4 5 6 7 8 9 10 11 12 13 14 15 16 17 18 19 20 21
(Adult to initial number representing the number of times quoted.)

Certification

I_____hereby certify that_____has quoted
this principle from memory 21 times, and is therefore entitled to the
<u>perseverance bonus</u> of $_____.

_____
Signature

WORK ETHIC

Is

The practice of

Working first

And

Playing later.

<u>Wisdom Payment Chart</u>

Every time you quote this principle from memory, you will earn_____.

(5c, 10c, 25c, etc.)

1 2 3 4 5 6 7 8 9 10 11 12 13 14 15 16 17 18 19 20 21

(Adult to initial number representing the number of times quoted.)

<u>Certification</u>

I_____hereby certify that_____has quoted this principle from memory 21 times, and is therefore entitled to the <u>perseverance bonus</u> of $_____.

_____

Signature

"IF ANY OF YOU LACKS WISDOM,
HE SHOULD ASK GOD, WHO
GIVES GENEROUSLY TO ALL
WITHOUT FINDING FAULT, AND
IT WILL BE GIVEN HIM."

JAMES 1:5 (NIV)

STUDY PAGE

1. **Accountability** is being good for your word.

2. **Action** is doing something, even if you are not completely sure.

3. **Awareness** is being tuned into the world around you.

4. **Character** is the drive to finish what you start, even if it is difficult.

5. **Consistency** is doing the same things the same way.

6. **Courage** is doing what you are supposed to do, even when you are afraid to do it.

7. **Courtesy** is treating others in a respectful manner.

8. **Creativity** is finding new ways to get things done.

9. **Discipline** is doing what you are supposed to do, even when you don't feel like doing it.

10. **Edification** is building another person up.

11. **Enthusiasm** is the positive energy that comes from God within.

12. **Excellence** is doing things in an outstandingly good way.

13. **Fairness** is giving to each person what they have earned.

14. **Faith** is knowing that you will have what you want, even if you don't see it yet.

15. **Forgiveness** is not holding other people's bad behavior against them.

16. **Giving** is willingly letting another person have what belongs to you.

17. **Honesty** is being truthful in thought, word, and deed.

18. **Humility** is not making a big deal of yourself.

19. **Inner Strength** is knowing that you have what it takes, and acting on it.

20. **Integrity** is doing the right thing, even if it costs you.

21. **Justice** is giving to each person what they deserve.

22. **Knowledge** is having the information you need to do what you are supposed to do.

23. **Laughter** is the sound that comes from making someone happy.

24. **Love** is giving of yourself.

25. **Mentorship** is learning from another person's experience.

26. **Mercy** is being kind to someone who is less fortunate that yourself.

27. **Modesty** is not making a big deal of your success.

28. **Obedience** is doing what you are told, when you are told, and the first time you are told.

29. **Optimism** is believing in a positive outcome.

30. **Passion** is doing what you do with all your heart.

31. **Patience** is waiting for what you want, know you will get it.

32. **Perseverance** is persistence under the most sever conditions.

33. **Persistence** is trying one more time than you fail.

34. **Politeness** is doing and saying things in a kind way.

35. **Positive** Mental Attitude is knowing that everything is going to be all right.

36. **Prudence** is using good judgement.

37. **Punctuality** is being where you need to be on time.

38. **Respect** is recognizing the greatness in yourself and others.

39. **Responsibility** is looking to yourself to get something done.

40. **Sacrifice** is giving up something important to you, for something better.

41. **Self Esteem** is seeing yourself the way God sees you.

42. **Serendipity** is the unexpected blessing that God gives you for trying.

43. **Service** is doing something to help others.

44. **Submission** is allowing another person to lead you.

45. **Success** is dreaming and making your dreams come true.

46. **Transparency** is being the same person in public that you are in private.

47. **Understanding** is making sense out of knowledge.

48. **Vision** is seeing things that don't exist now, but will exist in the future, as a result of your hard work and God's help.

49. **Wisdom** is knowing what to do and doing it when you are supposed to do it; and knowing what not to do and NOT doing it.

50. **Work Ethic** is the practice of working first, and playing later.

ABOUT THE AUTHOR

Rev. Everton (Tony) Robinson has worked over 40 years in church leadership as a minister, elder, worship leader and steward, and has shared the principles of wisdom through his work with various church-based organizations. In addition, he has mentored a variety of spiritual leaders and has conducted marriage enrichment programs that have been instrumental in saving many marriages.

Rev. Robinson, the son of a minister, spent most of his childhood and formative years attending church. Robinson left the church during his mid-teens and remained "unchurched" until his mid-twenties. However, after coming to the realization that his own skill, business acumen and intellect were not enough—and that he needed a relationship with God--he began to study the Bible with a true passion, and became fascinated with the concept of wisdom. He embraced wisdom, and decided to make it a way of life for himself, his wife, and his future children. Sometime later, Robinson attended a business seminar in which he learned principles of success. He was so inspired by the success principles that he began to identify key principles of wisdom to teach to his children. With the encouragement of his wife, Judith, Rev. Robinson compiled the 50 principles presented in this book.

Rev. Robinson is currently an Ordained Elder in the African Methodist Episcopal Church in Los Angeles, California; an Investment Advisor with FIT Planning Group; an entrepreneur in the E-Commerce business space; a songwriter, and a family man, residing in Buena Park, California. He may be reached for personal appearances at trobinson1952@gmail.com.